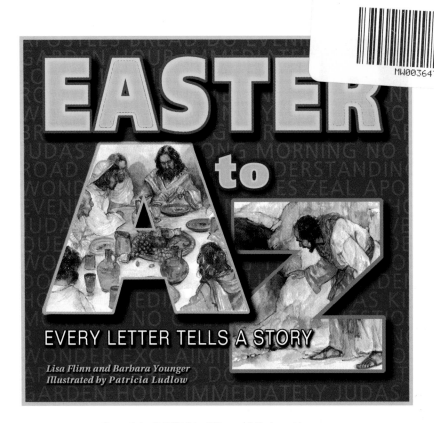

EASTER to A Z

EVERY LETTER TELLS A STORY

Lisa Flinn and Barbara Younger
Illustrated by Patricia Ludlow

Copyright © 2002 Lisa Flinn and Barbara Younger
All rights reserved.

ISBN: 0-687-026849

Scripture quotations marked CEV are from the Contemporary English Version, Copyright © American Bible Society, 1995. Used by permission.

Scripture quotations marked NRSV are from the New Revised Standard Version Bible, copyright © 1989, by the Division of Christian Education of the National Council of the Churches of Christ in the U.S.A. Used by permission.

Scripture quotations marked NCV are from the New Century Version Bible, copyright © 1986 by Worthy Publishing, Fort Worth Texas, 76137. Used by permission.

Scripture quotations marked NIV are from the Holy Bible, New International Version. Copyright © 1973, 1978, 1984, by International Bible Society. Used by permission of Zondervan. All rights reserved.

02 03 04 05 06 07 08 09 10 11– 10 9 8 7 6 5 4 3 2 1
MANUFACTURED IN THE UNITED STATES OF AMERICA

Abingdon Press

$\mathcal{A}$ is for Apostles who gathered in the room.

$\mathcal{B}$ is for the Bread that Jesus broke for them.

$\mathcal{C}$ is for the Cup filled with the fruit of the vine.

$\mathcal{D}$ is for "Do this in remembrance of me."

$\mathcal{E}$ is for the Evening of that Last Supper.

$\mathcal{F}$ is for Foretelling what was to come to pass.

When the time came, Jesus and the apostles were sitting at the table.

Jesus took some bread. He thanked God for it, broke it, and gave it to the apostles. Then Jesus said, "This bread is my body that I am giving for you. Do this in remembrance of me." In the same way, after supper, Jesus took the cup and said, "This cup shows the new agreement that God makes with his people. This new agreement begins with my blood which is poured out for you."

Luke 22:14, 19-20 NCV

3

G is for the Garden where they went to pray.

H is for "the Hour has come."

I is for Immediately a hostile crowd appeared.

J is for Judas who traded friendship for silver.

K is for the Kiss that betrayed God's Son.

L is for the Long dreadful night.

They went to a place called Gethsemane, and Jesus said to his disciples, "Sit here while I pray."
. . . Judas, one of the Twelve, appeared. With him was a crowd armed with swords and clubs, sent from the chief priests, the teachers of the law, and the elders.
Going at once to Jesus, Judas said, "Rabbi!" and kissed him. The men seized Jesus and arrested him.

Mark 14:32, 43, 45-46 NIV

5

M is for the Morning when the rooster crowed.

N is for "No, I don't know him."

. . . A servant girl of the high priest came up and saw Peter warming himself by the fire. She stared at him and said, "You were with Jesus from Nazareth!"

Peter replied, "That isn't true!" . . . He went out to the gate, and a rooster crowed.

The servant girl saw Peter again and said to the people standing there, "This man is one of them!"

"No, I'm not!" Peter replied.

A little while later some of the people said to Peter, "You certainly are one of them."

[Peter said,] "I don't even know the man you're talking about!"

Right away the rooster crowed a second time. Then Peter remembered that Jesus had told him, "Before a rooster crows twice, you will say three times that you don't know me." So Peter started crying.

Mark 14:66-72 CEV

7

O is for the handing Over of Jesus, from Pilot to Herod and back.

P is for the People shouting, "Crucify him!"

Q is for the Questions left unanswered.

Everyone in the council got up and led Jesus off to Pilate.

Pilate told the chief priests and the crowd, "I don't find him guilty of anything."

But they all kept on saying, "He has been teaching and causing trouble all over Judea. He started in Galilee and has now come all the way here."

When Pilate learned that Jesus came from the region ruled by Herod, he sent him to Herod, who was in Jerusalem at that time.

Herod asked him a lot of questions, but Jesus did not answer.

Herod and his soldiers made fun of Jesus and insulted him. They put a fine robe on him and sent him back to Pilate

Luke 23:1, 4-7, 9, 11 CEV

9

R is for the Road to the Place of the Skull.

S is for the Savior who died on the cross.

The soldiers took charge of Jesus. Carrying his own cross, Jesus went out to a place called The Place of the Skull. There they nailed Jesus to the cross.

John 19:16b-18a NCV

Jesus knew that everything had been done.

John 19:28a NCV

He bowed his head and died.

John 19: 30 NCV

𝒯 is for the Tomb where they laid him that day.

After these things, Joseph of Arimathea . . . asked Pilate to let him take away the body of Jesus. Pilate gave him permission; so he came and removed his body. Nicodemus, who had at first come to Jesus by night, also came, bringing a mixture of myrrh and aloes, weighing about a hundred pounds. They took the body of Jesus and wrapped it with the spices in linen cloths, according to the burial custom of the Jews. Now there was a garden in the place where he was crucified, and in the garden there was a new tomb in which no one had ever been laid. And so, because it was the Jewish day of Preparation, and the tomb was nearby, they laid Jesus there.

John 19:38-42 NRSV

U is for Understanding the angel's words, "He is not here; he has risen."

V is for the Victory of life over death.

W is for the Wonder of the empty tomb.

On the first day of the week, very early in the morning, the women took the spices they had prepared and went to the tomb. They found the stone rolled away from the tomb, but when they entered, they did not find the body of the Lord Jesus. While they were wondering about this, suddenly two men in clothes that gleamed like lightning stood beside them. In their fright the women bowed down with their faces to the ground, but the men said to them, "Why do you look for the living among the dead? He is not here; he has risen!"

It was Mary Magdalene, Joanna, Mary the mother of James, and the others with them who told this to the apostles. But they did not believe the women because their words seemed to them like nonsense. Peter, however, got up and ran to the tomb. Bending over, he saw the strips of linen lying by themselves, and he went away, wondering to himself what had happened.

Luke 24:1-6, 10-12 NIV

𝒳 is for eXclaiming the good news then and now.

𝒴 is for "Yes!" we believe.

𝒵 is for the Zeal of those who were there and of Easter people everywhere.

Go therefore and make disciples of all nations, baptizing them in the name of the Father and of the Son and of the Holy Spirit, and teaching them to obey everything that I have commanded you. And remember, I am with you always, to the end of the age."

Matthew 28:19-20 NRSV